Way Cool

Italian

Phrase Book

Third Edition

JANE WIGHTWICK

New York Chicago San Francisco Lisbon London Madrid Mexico City
Milan New Delhi San Juan Seoul Singapore Sydney Toronto

About this book

Jane Wightwick
had the idea

Wina Gunn
wrote the pages

Leila & Zeinah Gaafar
(aged 10 and 12) drew the
first pictures in
each chapter

Robert Bowers
(aged 52) drew the other
pictures, and designed
the book

Marc Vitale
did the Italian stuff

Important things that
must be included

3

What's inside

Making friends

How to be cool with the group

Wanna play?

Our guide to joining in everything from hide-and-seek to the latest electronic game

Feeling hungry

Order your favorite foods or go local

Looking good

Make sure you keep up with all those essential fashions

Hanging out

At the pool, beach, or theme park – don't miss out on the action

Pocket money

Spend it here!

Grown-up talk

blah! blah! blah! blah!

If you really, really have to!

Extra stuff

All the handy things – numbers, months, time, days of the week

my big brother il mio fratello grande

🫦 eel meeyo fratel-loh granday

dad
papà
🫦 pa-pah

grandpa
nonno
🫦 non-noh

grandma
nonna
🫦 non-nah

mom mamma
🫦 mam-mah

my little sister
la mia sorellina
🫦 la meeya
sorel-leenah

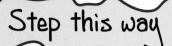
Step this way

stepfather/stepmother
patrigno/matrigna
🗣 patreenio/matreenia

stepson/stepdaughter
figliastro/figliastra
🗣 feelyeeastroh/
feelyeeastrah

stepbrother/stepsister
fratellastro/sorellastra
🗣 fratel-lastroh/
sorel-lastrah

Hi!
Ciao!
🗣 chee-ow

What's your name?
Come ti chiami?
🗣 komay tee kee-amee

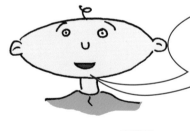

My name's ...
Mi chiamo ...
🗣 mee kee-amoh

The word *ciao* means "hello" <u>and</u> "goodbye" – it's such a famous word you might already use it with your English friends. You can say *Ciao, come va?* (*chee-ow, komay vah*, "Hi, how's it going?") or *Ciao, ci vediamo!* (*chee-ow, chee vaydee-amoh*, "Bye, see you later!")

from Canada
dal Canada
👄 dal kana-da

from Ireland
dall'Irlanda
👄 dal-leerlanda

from Scotland
dalla Scozia
👄 dal-la skotseea

from Wales
dal Galles
👄 dal gal-les

from the U.S.
dagli Stati Uniti
👄 dalyee statee uneetee

from England
dall'Inghilterra
👄 dal-lingilter-ra

10

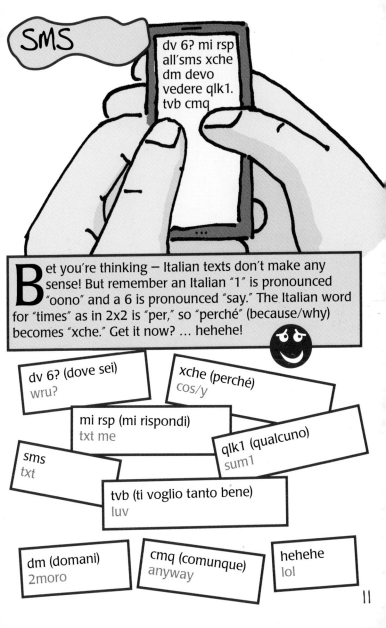

SMS

> dv 6? mi rsp all'sms xche dm devo vedere qlk1. tvb cmq

Bet you're thinking — Italian texts don't make any sense! But remember an Italian "1" is pronounced "oono" and a 6 is pronounced "say." The Italian word for "times" as in 2x2 is "per," so "perché" (because/why) becomes "xche." Get it now? … hehehe!

dv 6? (dove sei)
wru?

xche (perché)
cos/y

mi rsp (mi rispondi)
txt me

qlk1 (qualcuno)
sum1

sms
txt

tvb (ti voglio tanto bene)
luv

dm (domani)
2moro

cmq (comunque)
anyway

hehehe
lol

How old are you?
Quanti anni hai?
👄 kwantee an-nee eye

12 years old
Dodici anni
👄 dodeechee an-nee

Happy birthday!
Buon compleanno!
👄 boo-on komplayan-no

What's your star sign?
Di che segno sei?
👄 dee kay sayneeo say

When's your birthday?
Quando è il tuo compleanno?
👄 kwando ay eel too-oh komplayan-no

Star signs

AQUARIUS
Jan. 21 – Feb. 19
Acquario 💋 ak-kwareaoh

PISCES
Feb. 20 – Mar. 20
Pesci 💋 payshi

ARIES
Mar. 21 – Apr. 20
Ariete 💋 aree-aytay

TAURUS
Apr. 21 – May. 21
Toro 💋 toroh

GEMINI
May 22 – June 21
Gemelli 💋 jaymel-lee

CANCER
June 22 – July 23
Cancro 💋 kankroh

LEO
July 24 – Aug. 23
Leone 💋 layonay

VIRGO
Aug. 24 – Sep. 23
Vergine 💋 vayrjeenay

LIBRA
Sep. 24 – Oct. 23
Bilancia 💋 beelancheea

SCORPIO
Oct. 24 – Nov. 22
Scorpione 💋 skorpeeonay

SAGITTARIUS
Nov. 23 – Dec. 21
Sagittario 💋 sajeet-taraeo

CAPRICORN
Dec. 22 – Jan. 20
Capricorno 💋 kapreecorno

13

soccer il calcio
🫦 kalchee-oh

rollerblading
il pattinaggio
🫦 pat-teenaj-jeeoh

music
la musica
🫦 moozikah

electronic games
i giochi elettronici
🫦 ee jee-okee aylet-tr-roneechee

tv
la tele
🫦 la taylay

comics
i fumetti
🫦 ee foomayt-tee

school la scuola
🫦 la skwolah

spiders i ragni
🫦 ee ranyee

15

What's ...?

Qual è ...?

👄 kwalay

your favorite group

il tuo complesso preferito

👄 eel too-oh komples-soh pray-fayreetoh

your favorite color

il tuo colore preferito

👄 eel too-oh koloray pray-fayreetoh

Page 69

your favorite game

il tuo gioco preferito

👄 eel too-oh jee-okoh pray-fayreetoh

your favorite food
il tuo cibo preferito
👄 eel too-oh cheeboh
pray-fayreetoh

your favorite ring tone
la tua suoneria preferita
👄 la too-ah soo-onereeyah
pray-fayreetah

your favorite animal
il tuo animale preferito
👄 eel too-oh aneemalay
pray-fayreetoh

your favorite team
la tua squadra preferita
👄 la too-ah
skwadra pray-
fayreetah

Talk about your pets

He's hungry
È affamato
ay afah-maytoh

Can I pet your dog?
Posso accarezzare il tuo cane?
possoh akaraytzaray eel too-oh kanay

She's sleeping
Sta dormendo
stah dormendoh

Do you have any pets?
Hai qualche animali?
eye kwalkay aneemah-lee

dog
il cane

 eel kanay

cat
il gatto

 eel gat-toh

snake
il serpente

eel sairpayntay

guinea pig
il porcellino d'India

 eel porchel-leenoh

deendeea

hamster
il criceto

 eel crichaytoh

budgie
il pappagallino

 eel pap-

pagal-leenoh

My Little doggy goes *"bau bau"*!

An Italian doggy doesn't say "woof, woof," it says *bau, bau* (*baoo, baoo*). An Italian bird says *pio, pio* (*pee-o, pee-o*) and a "cock-a-doodle-do" in Italian chicken-speak is *chic-chirichì* (*keek-kee ree-kee*). But a cat does say "miao" and a cow "moo" whether they're speaking Italian or English!

IT

il computer

👄 eel "computer"

Way unfair!

Italian children hardly ever have to wear uniform to school nowadays (but in primary school they used to wear overalls, white with a big blue bow for girls and blue with a big white bow for boys!). Summer holidays are very long, sometimes even up to 12 weeks. But before you turn green with envy, you might not like the dreaded **ripetizioni** (*reepay-teetsee-onee*) or "vacation classes," which you have to take if you fail your end-of-year exams. And if your marks are really bad the teachers could make you repeat the whole year with your little sister!

Talk about your phone

That's ancient
Che vecchio!
👄 kay vekyoh

I've run
out of credit
Ho finito i soldi
👄 oh fineetoh
ee soldee

What's your phone like?
Com'è il tuo telefonino?
👄 komay eel too-oh
taylayfoneenoh

Lucky!
Sei troppo fortunato!
👄 say troppo
fortoon-atoh

What a great ring tone!
Che bella la tua suoneria!
👄 kay bella lah too-ah
soo-onereeyah

23

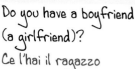

Gossip

Can you keep a secret?

Sai mantenere un segreto?

👄 sah-ee mantaynayray oon saygretoh

Do you have a boyfriend (a girlfriend)?

Ce l'hai il ragazzo (la ragazza)?

👄 chay l'eye eel ragatsoh (lah ragatsah)

An OK guy/An OK girl

Un tipo simpatico/Una tipa simpatica 👄 oon teepo seempateekoh/oona teepa seempateekah

Way bossy!

Che prepotente!

👄 kay praypotayntay

He's nutty/She's nutty!

È uno svitato/È una svitata!

👄 ay oono sveetatoh/ay oona sveetatah

svitato means 'unscrewed'!

What a complainer!

Che lagna!

👄 kay laneea

24

You won't make many friends saying this!

Bug off!
Levati dai piedi!
👄 layvatee die peeaydee
That means "get off my feet"!

Shut up! Sta' zitto!
👄 stah dzeet-toh

If you're fed up with someone, and you want to say something like "you silly …!" or "you stupid …!" you can start with **testa di** … (which actually means "head of …") and add anything you like. The most common are:

Cabbage head!
Testa di cavolo!
taystah dee kavoloh

Turnip head!
Testa di rapa!
taystah dee rapah

Take your pick. You could also start with **pezzo di** … ("piece of …") and say **pezzo d'idiota!** (*paytso deedee-otah*). You don't need a translation here, do you?

25

You might have to say

Fudge!
Uffa!
🗣 oof-fah

Rats!
Mannaggia!
🗣 man-naj-jeeah

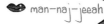

That's not funny
Non fa ridere nessuno
🗣 non fah reedayray nesoonoh

That's plenty!
Basta così!
🗣 bastah kozee

I'm fed up
Sono stufo! (boys)
Sono stufa! (girls)
🗣 sono stoofoh

sono stoofah

26

Stop it!

Smettila!

 smayt-teela

I want to go home!

Voglio tornare a casa!

 volyoh tornaray ah

kaza

I don't care

Non me ne importa niente

 non may nay importah neeayntay

At last!

Finalmente!

 feenalmayntay

Saying goodbye

What's your address?
Qual è il tuo indirizzo?

🫦 kwalay eel too-oh eendeereetso

Here's my address
Ecco il mio indirizzo

🫦 ekko eel meeo eendeereetso

Come to visit me
Vieni a trovarmi

🫦 vee-aynee ah trovarmee

il lettore
🗣 eel laytoray

lo yo-yo
🗣 loh "yo-yo"

il telefonino
🗣 eel taylayfoneenoh

WANNA PLAY?

Do you want to play ...?
Vuoi giocare ...?
🫧 voo-oi jokaray

... foos-ball?
... a calcetto?
🫧 ah kal-chayt-toh

... cards?
... a carte?
🫧 ah kartay

... on the computer?
... al computer?
🫧 al komputer

... hangman?
... all'impiccato?
🫧 al-leempeek-katoh

... hide and seek?
... a nascondino?
ah naskondeenoh

... catch?
... a palla?
ah pal-lah

Not now
Adesso no
adays-so noh

Yeah, let's!
Sì, giochiamo!
see, jeeokee-amoh

33

Fancy a game of **leap the foal** or **pretty statues**?

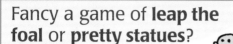

In Italy, tag is called **chiapparello** (*kiap-parel-loh*), which sort of means "catchy-poos"! And instead of leap frog, Italian children play leap "foal" – **la cavallina** (*lah caval-leenah*). Another very popular game is **belle statuine** (*bellay statoo-eenay*) or "pretty statues," which is similar to "big bad wolf." When someone is standing around doing nothing, Italians will often ask "Are you playing pretty statues?" – **Fai la bella statuina?** (*fie lah bellah statoo-eenah*).

Can my friend play too?
Può giocare anche il mio amico?
💋 poo-o jeeokaray ankay eel mee-yo ameekoh?

I have to ask my parents
Devo chiedere ai miei
💋 dayvoh keeaydayray eye mee-ay

35

Who dares?

You're it!
Stai sotto tu!
👄 sty sot-to too

Race you!
Facciamo una corsa?
👄 facheeamoh oona korsah

I'm first
Sono primo io (boy)
Sono prima io (girl)
👄 sonoh preemoh eeo
sonoh preemah eeo

Electronic games

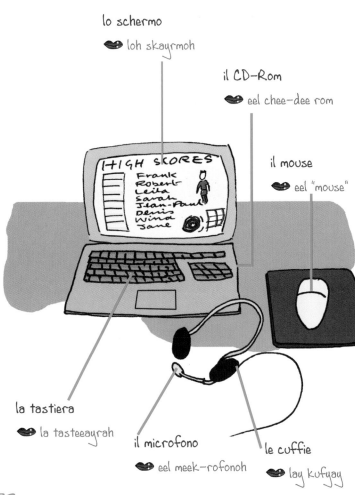

lo schermo
🗣 loh skayrmoh

il CD-Rom
🗣 eel chee-dee rom

il mouse
🗣 eel "mouse"

la tastiera
🗣 la tasteeayrah

il microfono
🗣 eel meek-rofonoh

le cuffie
🗣 lay kufyay

HIGH SCORES

Frank
Robert
Leila
Sarah
Jean-Paul
Denis
Wina
Jane

Show me
Fammi vedere
 fam-mee vaydayray

What do I do?
Che devo fare?
kay dayvoh faray

Am I dead?
Sono morto?
sonoh
mortoh

Shoot-em-up!
Spara!
sparah

How many lives do I have?
Quante vite ho?
kwantay veetay oh

How many levels are there?
Quanti livelli ci sono?
kwantee leevayl-lee chee sonoh

39

It's virtual fun!

Do you have WiFi?
Hai WiFi?

👄 eye "weefee"

Make sure you say it like this to avoid blank looks!

Send me a message.
Mandami un messaggio.

How do i join?
Come m'iscrivo?

I'm not old enough.
Non sono grande abbastanza.

I'm not allowed.
Non mi è permesso.

I don't know who you are.
Non so chi sei.

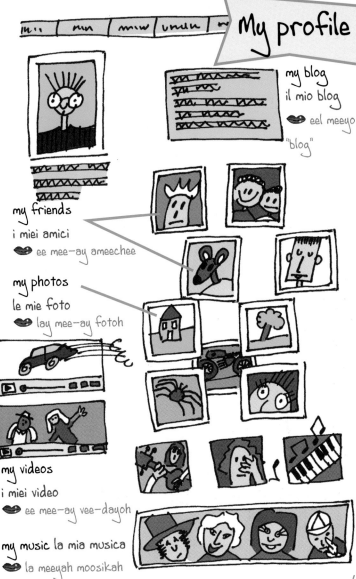

My profile

my blog
il mio blog
💋 eel meeyo "blog"

my friends
i miei amici
💋 ee mee-ay ameechee

my photos
le mie foto
💋 lay mee-ay fotoh

my videos
i miei video
💋 ee mee-ay vee-dayoh

my music la mia musica
💋 la meeyah moosikah

41

Non couch-potato activities!

trampolining

il trampolino

eel trampoleenoh

tennis

il tennis

eel ten-nees

bowling

il bowling

eel booleeng

swimming

il nuoto

eel noo-oto

hockey

l'hockey

👄 lok-kay

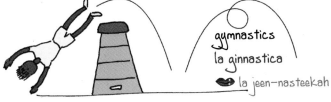

gymnastics

la ginnastica

👄 la jeen-nasteekah

ballet

la danza classica

👄 la dantsa klas-seekah

basketball

la pallacanestro

👄 la pal-lakanaystroh

and, of course, we haven't forgotten *"il calcio"*… (P.T.O.)   43

soccer

cleats

gli scarponcini

🗣 lyee skarponcheenee

soccer gear

la divisa da calcio

🗣 lah deeveezah dah kalcheeo

ref

l'arbitro

🗣 larbeetroh

shin pads

i parastinchi

🗣 ee parasteenkee

Good save!

Ben parato!

🗣 ben paratoh

44

Pass! Passa!

🗣 pas–sah

defender
il difensore
🗨 eel deefen-soray

attacker
l'attaccante
🗨 lattak-kantay

Foul!
Fallo!
🗨 fal-loh

He pushed me!
Mi ha dato uno spintone!
🗨 mee ah dato oono
speentonay

Penalty!
Rigore!
🗨 reegoray

Goal!
Gol!
🗨 gol

46

Keeping the others in line

Not like that!

Così no!

🗣 kozee noh

You cheat! Sei un imbroglione! (boys only)

Sei un'imbrogliona! (girls only)

🗣 say oon eembrolyee-onay

say oon eembrolyee-onah

I'm not playing anymore

Non gioco più

🗣 non jeeoko peeoo

It's not fair!

Non vale!

🗣 non valay

Stop it!

Smettila!

🗣 smayt-teela

Showing off

... do a handstand?
... fare la verticale?
🗣 faray la
vayrteecalay

Can you ...
Sai ...
🗣 sah-ee

Look at me!
Guardatemi!
🗣 gooardataymee

... do a cartwheel?
... fare la ruota?
🗣 ... fare la ruota?

... do this?
... fare questo?
🗣 faray kwaystoh

Tongue tied

Impress your Italian friends with this!

Show off to your new Italian friends by practicing this **scioglilingua** (*shee-olyeleen-gooa*), or tongue twister:

Sopra la panca la capra campa, sotto la panca la capra crepa.

Soprah la pankah la kaprah kampah, sot-toh la pankah la kaprah kraypah

(This means "On the bench the goat lives, under the bench the goat dies.")

Then see if they can do as well with this English one:

"She sells seashells on the seashore, but the shells she sells aren't seashells, I'm sure."

49

For a rainy day

deck of cards

mazzo di carte

🫦 matso dee kartay

my deal/your deal

do io le carte/dai tu le carte

🫦 dahray eo lay kartay/ die too lay kartay

king

il re

🫦 eel ray

queen

la regina

🫦 la rayjeenah

jack

il fante

🫦 eel fantay

joker

il jolly

🫦 eel jol-lee

fiori

🫦 feeoree

cuori

🫦 koo-oree

picche

🫦 peek-kay

quadri

🫦 kwadree

Do you have the ace of swords?!

Y ou may see Italian children playing with a different pack of cards. There are only 40 cards instead of 52 and the suits are also different. Instead of clubs, spades, diamonds and hearts, there are gold coins (**denari** *daynaree*), swords (**spade** *spahday*), cups (**coppe** *koppay*) and sticks (**bastoni** *bastonee*).

chessboard la scacchiera
💋 la skak-keeayrah

l'alfiere
💋 lalfeeayray

il cavallo
💋 eel kaval-loh

il pedone
💋 eel paydonay

la torre 💋 lah torray

la regina
💋 lah rayjeeanah

il re 💋 eel ray

FEELING HUNGRY

hamburger
l'hamburger
👄 lamboorgir

fries
le patate fritte
👄 lay patatay freet-tay

ice cream
il gelato
👄 eel jaylatoh

Fries

Cola

coke
la cola
👄 la kolah

FEELING HUNGRY

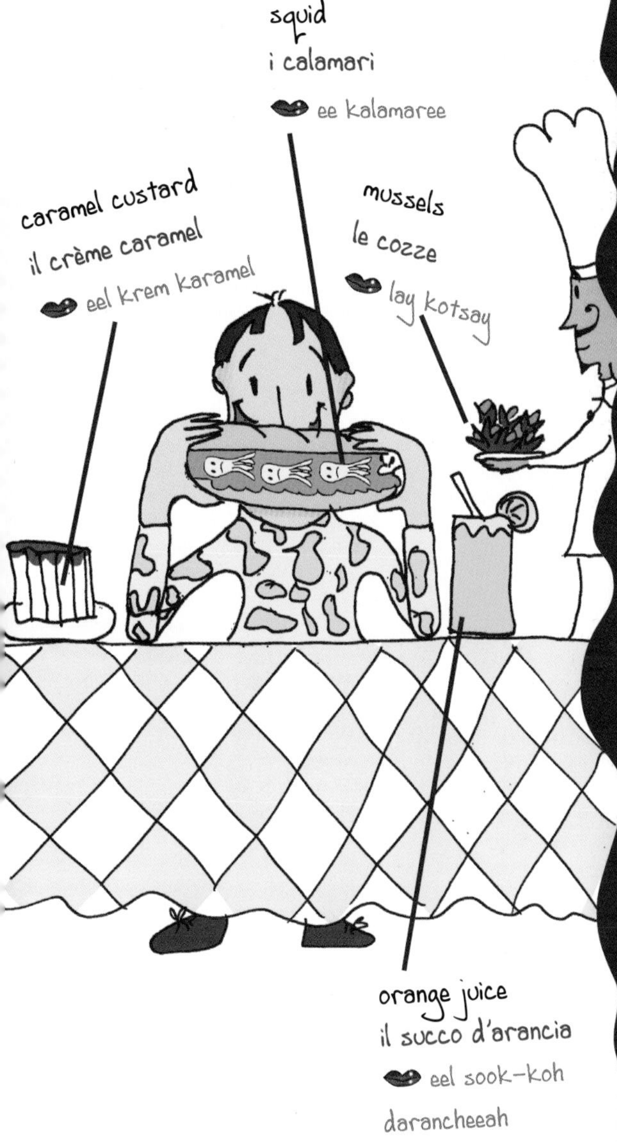

Grub

I'm starving

Ho una fame da lupo

👄 oh oona famay dah loopoh

That means "I have the hunger of a wolf!"

il lupo

Please can I have ...

Mi dà ...

👄 mee dah

54

... a croissant

... un cornetto

 oon cornayt-toh

... a chocolate pastry

... un pasticcino al cioccolato

 oon pasteech-cheeno al chok-kolatoh

... a sandwich

... un tramezzino

 oon tramay-dzeeno

... a slice of pizza

... un pezzo di pizza

 oon paytso dee peetsa

... a calzone

... un calzone

 oon caltsonay

In the winter, you can buy bags of delicious roasted chestnuts from street sellers, hot and ready to eat!

... a bag of chestnuts

un cartoccio di castagne

🗣 oon kartocheeo dee kastaneeay

Take-away pizza in Italy is often sold **al taglio** (*al talyee-oh*), which means it is cut into rectangular slices from a large baking sheet ... and you can buy as big a piece as you like. Another great midday snack is a **calzone** (*caltsonay*), which is a round pizza folded in half to look like a pastie, with all the juicy bits inside.

If you want something really cold and slushy in the summer you can ask for **una granita** (*oona graneetah*), which is crushed ice with fruit juice or syrup.

water

acqua

💋 akkwah

... a syrup

... uno sciroppo

💋 oonoh sheerop-poh

... a milkshake

... un frullato

💋 oon frool-latoh

If you're really lucky you might go to Italy during **Carnevale** in February. Adults and kids dress up in the weirdest costumes and everyone goes loopy for a few days. There are lots of special sticky cakes like **frappe** (*frappay*): big pastry bows dipped in icing sugar; and **castagnole** (*kastanyolay*): delicious fried balls of pastry covered in sugar.

You: Can I have some castagnole, Mom?

Mom: No. They'll make you fat and rot your teeth.

You: But I think it's good to experience a foreign culture through authentic local food.

Mom: Oh, all right then.

Pasta, Pasta, Pasta!

Italians, especially those from Naples, claim to have invented pasta (we know it really grows on trees!). There are lots of different types of pasta and just as many, if not more, different sauces to go with them, including a sauce made with squid ink! You have probably heard of **spaghetti** and **tagliatelle**, but what about these:

penne (quills)

farfalle (butterflies)

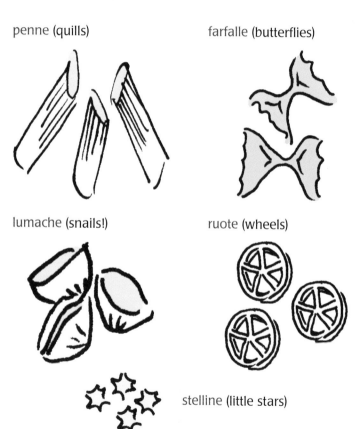

lumache (snails!)

ruote (wheels)

stelline (little stars)

Parties

balloon il palloncino

🗨 eel paloncheeno

Can I have some more?

Potrei averne un altro po'?

🗨 potray avairnay oon altroh po

This is for you

Questo è per te

🗨 kwaysto ay payr tay

party hat

il cappello da festa

🗨 eel kap-pello dah festa

What do Italian children play at birthday parties?

Pasta parcel!

61

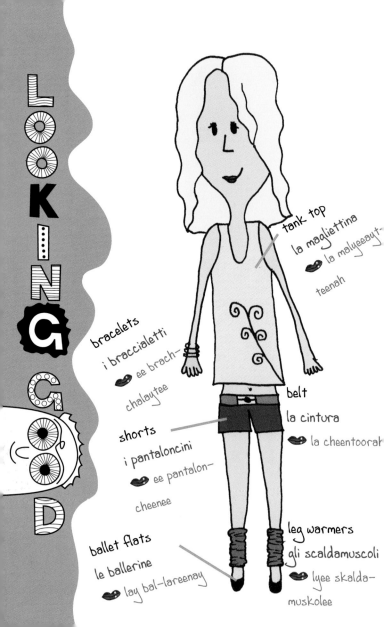

LOOKING GOOD

tank top
la magliettina
💋 la malyeeayt-
teenah

bracelets
i braccialetti
💋 ee brach-
chalaytee

belt
la cintura
💋 la cheentoorah

shorts
i pantaloncini
💋 ee pantalon-
cheenee

ballet flats
le ballerine
💋 lay bal-lareenay

leg warmers
gli scaldamuscoli
💋 lyee skalda-
muskolee

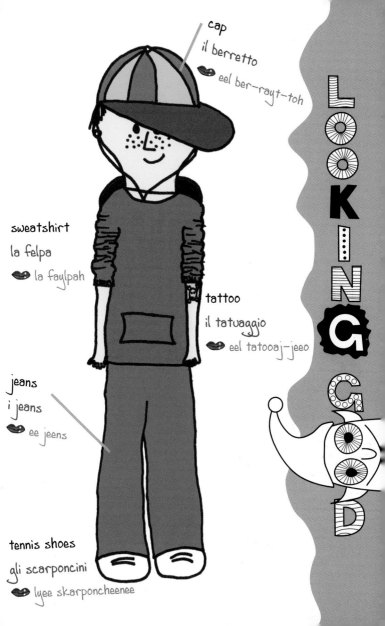

cap
il berretto
🗣 eel ber-rayt-toh

sweatshirt
la felpa
🗣 la faylpah

tattoo
il tatuaggio
🗣 eel tatooaj-jeeo

jeans
i jeans
🗣 ee jeens

tennis shoes
gli scarponcini
🗣 lyee skarponcheenee

LOOKING GOOD

Clothes

jeans
i jeans
👄 ee jeens

sweatshirt
la felpa
👄 la faylpah

T-shirt
la maglietta
👄 lah malyeeayt-tah

soccer jersey
la maglietta da calcio
👄 lah malyeeayt-tah da calcheeo

tennis shoes
gli scarponcini
👄 lyee skarponcheenee

dress

il vestito

👄 eel vaysteetoh

skirt

la gonna

👄 la gon-nah

pants

i pantaloni

👄 ee pantalonee

shorts

i pantaloncini

👄 ee pantaloncheenee

shoes

e scarpe

👄 lay skarpay

65

She's got an orange hair!
There are lots of double letters in Italian. Saying the double letter properly can be very important. For example, a hat is **un cappello** (*oon cap-payl-loh*), with two "p"s, but a hair is **un capello** (*oon capayl-lo*).

spotted

a pois

👄 ah pooah

flowery

a fiori

👄 ah feeoree

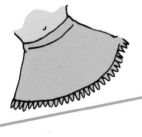

frilly

con i fronzoli

👄 kon ee frondzolee

glittery

luccicante

👄 luch-cheekantay

striped

a strisce

👄 ah streeshay

67

Make it up!

lip gloss
il lucidalabbra
👄 eel loocheedah-labrah

glitter gel
il gel luccicante
👄 eel "gel" luch-cheekantay

I need a mirror
Mi serve uno specchio
👄 mee servay oono spek-kyo

nail polish
lo smalto per le unghie
👄 lo smalto payr lay ungyay

earrings
gli orecchini
👄 lyee oraykeenee

eye shadow
l'ombretto
👄 lombrayt-to

Can I borrow your flat iron?
Me lo presti il tuo lisciacapelli?
👄 may lo prestee eel too-oh leesheeya-kapayllee

68

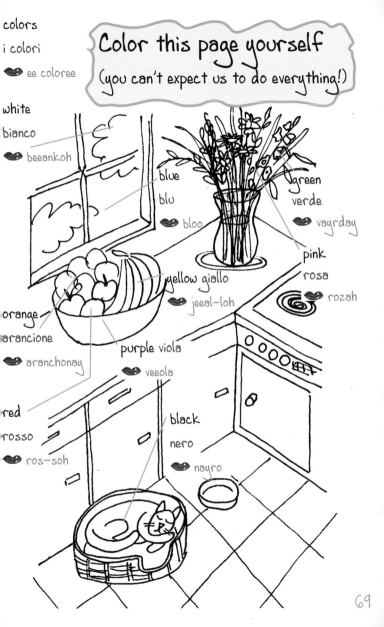

colors
i colori
👄 ee coloree

Color this page yourself
(you can't expect us to do everything!)

white
bianco
👄 beeankoh

blue
blu
👄 bloo

green
verde
👄 vayrday

pink
rosa
👄 rozah

yellow giallo
👄 jeeal-loh

orange
arancione
👄 aranchonay

purple viola
👄 veeola

red
rosso
👄 ros-soh

black
nero
👄 nayro

69

What should we do?

Che facciamo?

kay facheeamoh

Can I come too?

Vengo anch'io?

vayngo ankeeoh

Where do you lot hang out?

Dove v'incontrate?

dovay veenkontratay

That's really wicked

Che forte

kay fortay

I'm not allowed

Non mi lasciano

non mee lasheeanoh

Let's go back Torniamo indietro

👄 torneeamoh indeeaytroh

That gives me goose bumps (or "goose flesh" in Italian!)

Mi fa venire la pelle d'oca

👄 mee fah vayneeray la payl-lay dokah

I'm bored to death

Sto morendo dalla noia

👄 stoh morayndoh dal-la noya

That's a laugh

Quello è buffissimo

👄 kwel-lo ay boof-fees-seemoh

Beach bums

Can I borrow this?

Me lo presti?

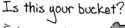 may loh praystee

Let's hit the beach

Tutti al mare

👄 toot-tee al maray

Is this your bucket?

È tuo questo secchiello?

👄 ay too-o kwestoh saykeeayl-lo

You can bury me

Mi puoi seppellire

👄 mee poo-oee sayp-payl-leeray

Stop throwing sand!

Smetti di tirare la sabbia!

👄 smayt-tee dee teeraray la sab-beeah

Mind my eyes!

Non mi buttare la sabbia negli occhi!

👄 non mee boot-taray la sab-beea nelyee ok-kee

74

sandcastle
il castello di sabbia
💋 eel kastayl-loh dee sab-beeah

sea
il mare
💋 eel maray

beach
la spiaggia
💋 la speeaj-jah

towel
l'asciugamano
💋 lashoogamanoh

bathing suit
il costume da bagno
💋 eel kostoomay dah banyeeoh

snorkel
il boccaglio
💋 eel bok-kaleeyo

bucket il secchiello
💋 eel sayk-keeayl-loh

shells
le conchiglie
💋 lay konkeelyeeay

shovel
la paletta
💋 la palayt-tah

75

It's going swimmingly!

How to make a splash in Italian!

Let's hit the swimming pool

Tutti in piscina

👄 toot–tee een peesheena

Can you swim (underwater)?

Sai nuotare (sott'acqua)?

👄 saee nwotaray (sot–takwah)

Me too/I can't

Anch'io/Io no

👄 ankeeo/eeo noh

I'm getting changed

Mi sto cambiando

👄 mee stoh kambeeandoh

Can you dive?

Ti sai tuffare?

👄 tee sah–ee
toof–faray

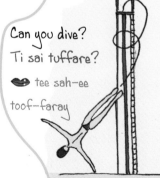

... backstroke

il dorso

🗨 eel dorsoh

Can you do ...?

Sai fare ...?

🗨 sah-ee faray

... butterfly

la farfalla

🗨 la farfal-la

... crawl

il stile libero

🗨 eel steelay leebayroh

breaststroke

la rana 🗨 la ranah
[which means "the frog," and, let's face it, that's what you look like!]

slide

lo scivolo

🗨 loh sheevoloh

goggles gli occhialini

🗨 lyee ok-keealeenee

77

Downtown

Do you know the way?
Sai la strada?

🗣 sah-ee la stradah

Let's ask
Chiediamo

🗣 kyee-aydeeamoh

Italy has a high-speed train called the **Pendolino**, which means "leaning over," because the carriages lean to the side when it speeds round bends. Persuade your parents to try it – it's better than a roller-coaster at the fun fair!

bus
l'autobus

🗣 laootoboos

Is it far?

È lontano?

👄 ay lontanoh

Are we allowed in here?

Possiamo entrare?

👄 pos-seeamoh ayntraray

car

la macchina

👄 lah mak-keenah

The "proper" Italian word for car is **automobile** (*aootomobeelay*) but you'll look much cooler if you say **macchina** (*mak-keenah*) or, if the car has seen better days, **macinino** (*macheeneenoh*). Use the cooler short words instead of those long untrendy ones the adults will try and make you say: **bici** (*beechee*) instead of **bicicletta**, **moto** instead of **motocicletta** and **bus** (*boos*) instead of **autobus**.

79

Park yourself here

swings le altalene
🗣 lay altalaynay

jungle gym il quadro svedese 🗣 eel kwadro zvedaysay

playground il parco giochi
🗣 eel parko jeeokee

grass il prato
🗣 eel prato

tree l'albero
🗣 lalbayro

slide
lo scivolo
🗣 lo sheevolo

80

park il parco 🗣 eel parko

Can we play ball games?

Giochiamo a palla?

🗣 jeeokee-ahmo a palla

merry-go-round

la giostra

🗣 la gee-ostra

sandbox

la sabbia

🗣 la sab-beeya

Can I have a go? Mi fai provare?

🗣 mee faee provaray

Picnics

I hate wasps

Odio le vespe

👄 odeeo lay

vayspay

Move over!

Fatti più in là!

👄 fat-tee

peeoo een lah

bread

il pane 👄 eel panay

ham il prosciutto

👄 eel proshoot-to

yogurt

lo yogurt

👄 loh yogoort

napkin

il tovagliolo

👄 eel tovalyeeolo

chips

le patatine

👄 lay patateenay

Let's sit here

Sediamoci qui

👄 saydeeamochee kwee

cheese

il formaggio

👄 eel formaj-jeeo

drinks

le bibite

🗨 lay beebeetay

knife

il coltello

🗨 eel koltayl-lo

spoon

il cucchiaio

🗨 eel kuk-keeayo

fork

la forchetta

🗨 la forkayt-tah

wasps

le vespe

🗨 lay vayspay

bees

le api

🗨 lay apee

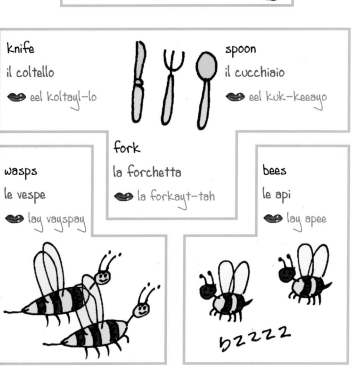

bzzzz

ants

le formiche

🗨 lay formeekay

Wake up, campers!

tent la tenda
🗣 la taynda

tent peg
il picchetto
🗣 eel peek-kayt-toh

camper van
il camper
🗣 eel "camper"

penknife
il coltellino svizzero
🗣 eel koltayl-leeno zveet-tzayro

sleeping bag il sacco a pelo
🗣 eel sakko a paylo

stove
il fornello
🗣 eel fornayllo

flashlight la torcia
🗣 la torcheeya

84

That tent's a palace!
Quella tenda è un palazzo!
👄 kwella taynda ay oon palat-zoh

campfire
il fuoco d'accampamento
👄 eel foo-oko dakampa-maynto

I've lost my flashlight
Ho perso la mia torcia
👄 oh payrso la meeya torcheeya

The showers are gross!
Le docce fanno schifo!
👄 lay dotchay fanno skeefo

Where does the garbage go?
Dove va la spazzatura?
👄 dovay vah la spatza-toorah

85

All the fun of the fair

Ferris wheel la ruota panoramica

🗣 la rwotah panorameeka

slide

lo scivolo

🗣 loh sheevolo

house of mirrors

la casa degli specchi

🗣 la kasah delyee spayk-kee

bumper cars

l'autoscontro

🗣 laootoskontro

Let's try this

Andiamo su questo

🗣 andeeamo soo kwesto

octopus

la giostra

🫦 la jeeostra

It's (too) fast

Va (troppo) forte

🫦 vah trop-po fortay

That's for babies

Quello è per i bambini

🫦 kwayl-lo ay payr ee bambeenee

Do you get wet here?

Qui ci si bagna?

🫦 kwee chee see banya

I'm not going on my own

Da solo/a non ci vado

🫦 dah solo/a non chee vado

87

Disco nights

mirror ball
la palla
specchiata
🗣 la palla
spayk-kyata

loudspeaker
la cassa
🗣 la kas-sa

Can I request a song?
Posso chiedere una canzone?
🗣 posso kee-ayderay oona kanzonay

The music is really lame
La musica è troppo noiosa
🗣 la mooseeka ay troppo noyosa

spotlight
lo spot
🗣 loh "spot"

DJ
il DJ
🗣 eel "DJ"

turntable la piatta-
forma girante 🗣 la
pyattaforma geerantay

How old do I need to be?

Quanti anni devo avere?

👄 kwantee annee dayvo averay

dance floor

la pista da ballo

👄 la peesta dah ballo

Shall we dance?

Balliamo?

👄 bal-lyahmo

I love this song!

Questa canzone mi fa impazzire!

👄 kwaysta kanzonay mee fah impat-zeeray

POCKET MONEY

candy
le caramelle
 lay karamayl-lay

T-shirts
le magliette
lay malyeeayt-tau

toys
i giocattoli
ee jeeokat-tolee

shop assistant
il commesso
eel kom-mays-so

books

i libri

 ee leebree

il mobile

eel "mobile"

pencils

le matite

lay mateetay

What does that sign say?

Macelleria

macelleria

butcher shop

👄 machayl-layreeah

pasticceria

cake shop

👄 pastee-chayreeah

Pasticceria

panetteria

bakery

👄 panayt-tayreea

Panetteria

negozio di dolciumi

candy store

👄 naygotseeo dee dolcheeoomee

cartoleria

office supplies

👄 kartolayreeah

Cartoleria

Fruttivendolo

fruttivendolo

fruit and vegetable store 👄 froot-teevayndoloh

Negozio di abbigliamento

negozio di abbigliamento

clothes shop

👄 naygotseeo dee ab-beelyeeamaynto

92

Do you have some dosh?

Ce l'hai qualche soldo?

💋 chay lie kwalkay soldo

I'm skint

Sono al verde

💋 sono al vayrday

I'm loaded

Sono ricco sfondato

💋 sono reek-ko sfondato

Here you go

Tieni

💋 teeaynee

This shop is weird!

Questo negozio è strano!

💋 kwesto naygotseeo ay stah-no

That's a bargain È un affare

💋 ay oon af-faray

It's a rip-off

Questi ti spellano!

💋 kwaystee tee spayl-lanoh

93

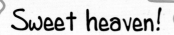

Sweet heaven!

I love this shop

Adoro questo negozio

 adohro kwesto naygotseeo

Let's get some candy

Prendiamo delle caramelle

 prayndeeamo dayllay karamayl-lay

Let's get some ice cream

Prendiamo un gelato

 prayndeeamo oon jaylatoh

lollipops

lecca lecca

 lek-kah

lek-kah

[that means "lick-lick"!]

a bar of chocolate

una tavoletta di cioccolata

 oona tavolayt-tah dee chok-kolatah

chewing gum

gomma da masticare

 gom-mah dah masteekaray

94

Baci Perugina
(bachee peroo-jeenah)
The most famous Italian chocolate has to be **baci Perugina** (literally "kisses"), nuggets of chocolate and nuts wrapped in silver paper with little romantic messages for that boy or girl you like!

carbone di zucchero
(carbonay dee dzook-kayro)!
Sugar coal. On 6th January, the Epiphany, Italian kids get presents, but those who have been naughty get coal! Actually this is black coal-shaped candy – phew!

pecorelle di zucchero
(paykorayl-lay dee dzook-kayro)
Forget the Easter eggs, try some 'little sugar sheep'!

Kinder sorpresa
(kinder sorpraysah)
You probably know these "Kinder Surprise" chocolate eggs with wicked little toys, but did you know they come from Italy?

Other things you could buy
(that won't ruin your teeth!)

What are you getting?
Tu che prendi?
🗨 too kay prayndee

That toy, please
Quel giocattolo, per favore
🗨 kwayl jeeokat-toloh payr favoray

Two postcards, please
Due cartoline, per favore
🗨 dooay kartoleenay payr favoray

This is garbage
Questa è robaccia
🗨 kwesta ay robach-cha

This is cool
Questo è eccezionale
🗨 kwesto ay echetseeonalay

96

I'm

getting ...

Io prendo ...

🗨 Io prendo ...

... a pen

... una penna

🗨 oona pen-nah

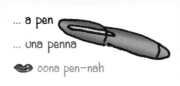

... stamps

... dei francobolli

🗨 day franko-bol-lee

... felt-tip pens

... dei pennarelli

🗨 day pen-narel-lee

... colored pencils

... delle matite colorate

🗨 dellay mateetay coloratay

... a key ring

... un portachiavi

🗨 oon portah-

kee-avee

... comics

... dei fumetti

🗨 day foomayt-tee

97

... a box ... una scatolina

🗣 oona skatoh-leenah

... a fridge magnet

... una calamita da frigorifero

🗣 oona kalameetah dah freego-reefayroh

... a necklace

... una collana

🗣 oona kollana

How much is that?

Quanto costa?

🗣 kwanto kostah

Italian kids, and adults, have always been mad about Disney comics. But did you know that most of the characters have Italian names you wouldn't recognize?
Mickey Mouse is **Topolino** ("little mouse"), Goofy is **Pippo**, Donald Duck is **Paperino** ("little duck") and Huey, Dewey, and Louie are **Qui, Quo, Qua**!

Money talks

How much pocket money do you get?

Quanta paghetta prendi?

🐛 kwantah pagayttah prayndee

I only have this much

Io ho solo questi soldi

🐛 eeo oh solo kwestee soldee

Can you lend me
ten euros?

Mi presti dieci euros?

🐛 mee praystee
deeaychee yooro

No way!

Neanche per sogno!

🐛 nayankay payr
sonyeeo

Money talk

Italian money is the **euro** (pronounced *ayoo-roh*).
A euro is divided into 100 **centesimi** (*chayntayseemee*).
Coins: 1, 2, 5, 10, 20, 50 **centesimi**
        1, 2 **euro**
Notes: 5, 10, 20, 50, 100 **euro**
Make sure you know how much you are spending before
you blow all your pocket money at once!

GROWN UP TALK

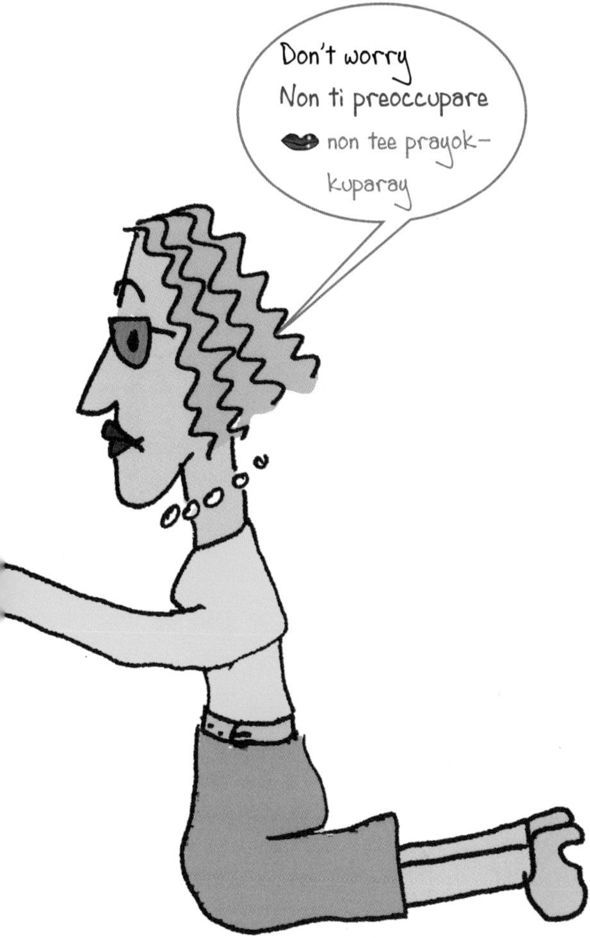

grown-up
adulto
adoolto

Help!

Something has broken
Si è rotto qualcosa
👄 see ay rot-to kwalkozah

Please
Per favore
👄 payr favoray

Can you help me?
Può aiutarmi?
👄 pwoh aeeootarmee

Where's the mailbox?
Dov'è la buca delle lettere?
👄 dovay lah booka dayl-lay
lay-tayray

Where are the toilets?
Dov'è il bagno?

👄 dovay eel banyeeo

I can't manage it

Non ci riesco

🗣 non chee ree-aysko

Could you pass me that?

Mi passi quello?

🗣 mee pas-see kwayl-lo

What time is it?

Che ore sono?

🗣 kay oray sonoh

Come and see

Vieni a vedere

🗣 veeaynee ah vaydayray

May I look at your watch?

Mi fa vedere sul suo orologio

🗣 mee fah vaydayray sool soo-o orolojeeo

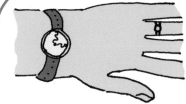

103

Lost for words

... my ticket

... il mio biglietto

👄 eel meeo

bilyee-ayt-to

I've lost ...

Ho perso ...

👄 oh payrso

... my phone

... il mio

telefonino

👄 eel meeo

taylayfoneenoh

... my parents

... i miei genitori

👄 ee meeay

jayneetoree

... my shoes
... le mie scarpe
👄 lay meeay skarpay

... my money ... i miei soldi
👄 ee meeay soldee

... my sweater
... la mia maglia
👄 lah meeah malyeeah

... my watch
... il mio orologio
👄 eel meeoh
orolojeeo

... my jacket ... la mia giacca
👄 lah meeah jeeak-kah

105

Adults only!

S how this page to adults
who can't seem to make
themselves clear (it happens).
They will point to a phrase,
you read what they mean,
and you should all understand
each other perfectly.

Non ti preoccupare
Don't worry

Siediti qui
Sit down here

Come ti chiami di nome e di cognome?
What's your name and surname?

Quanti anni hai?
How old are you?

Di dove sei?
Where are you from?

Dove sei alloggiato/a?
Where are you staying?

Cos'è che ti fa male?
Where does it hurt?

Sei allergico/a a qualcosa?
Are you allergic to anything?

È proibito
It's forbidden

Devi essere accompagnato/a da un adulto
You have to have an adult with you

Vado a cercare qualcuno che parli l'inglese
I'll get someone who speaks English

weather
il tempo
🫦 eel taympoh

numbers i numeri 🫦 ee noomayree

time

l'ora

lorah

EXTRA STUFF

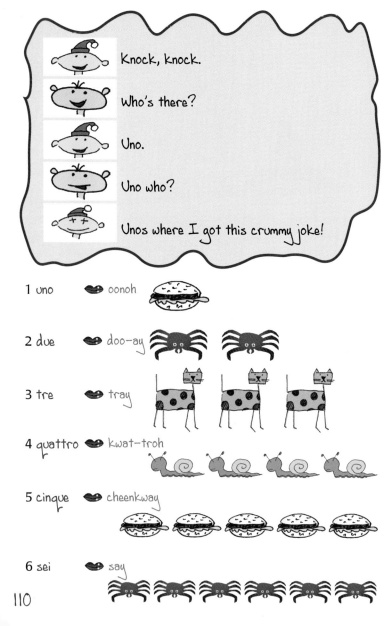

Knock, knock.

Who's there?

Uno.

Uno who?

Unos where I got this crummy joke!

1 uno 💋 oonoh

2 due 💋 doo-ay

3 tre 💋 tray

4 quattro 💋 kwat-troh

5 cinque 💋 cheenkway

6 sei 💋 say

7 sette
 sayt-tay

8 otto
 ot-toh

9 nove
novay

10 dieci
deeaychee

11 undici
oondeechee

12 dodici
dodeechee

13 tredici  traydeechee

14 quattordici  kwat-tordeechee

15 quindici  kweendeechee

16	sedici	*saydeechee*
17	diciassette	*deechas-set-tay*
18	diciotto	*deechot-toh*
19	diciannove	*dechan-novay*
20	venti	*vayntee*

If you want to say "twenty-two," "sixty-five," and so on, you can just put the two numbers together like you do in English:

| 22 | ventidue | *vaynteedooay* |
| 65 | sessantacinque | *sayss-santacheenkway* |

This works except if you're saying "twenty-one," "sixty-one" and so on. Then you need to remove the final letter from the first number:

| 21 | ventuno (not ventiuno) | *vayntoonoh* |
| 61 | sessantuno (not sessantauno) | *sayss-santoonoh* |

30	trenta	*trayntah*
40	quaranta	*kwarantah*
50	cinquanta	*cheenkwantah*
60	sessanta	*sayssayntah*
70	settanta	*sayt-tantah*
80	ottanta	*ot-tantah*
90	novanta	*novantah*
100	cento	*chentoh*

a thousand	mille	*meel-lay*
a million	un milione	*oon meel-lyonay*
a gazillion!	un fantastiliardo!	*oon fantasteeylardoh*

You might notice that Italians wave their hands a lot when they speak. What you won't realize is that not all flapping and waving means the same. Try looking out for some of these:

"What do you want?"

"Say that again"

"Are you crazy?"

"He's changed his mind"

March	marzo	*martsoh*
April	aprile	*apreelay*
May	maggio	*madjoh*

June	giugno	*joonyoh*
July	luglio	*loolyoh*
August	agosto	*agostoh*

September	settembre	*set-tembray*
October	ottobre	*ot-tobray*
November	novembre	*novembray*

December	dicembre	*deechaymbray*
January	gennaio	*jen-nayoh*
February	febbraio	*feb-brayoh*

primavera   *preemavayrah*

SPRING

estate   *estatay*

SUMMER

autunno   *owtoon-noh*

AUTUMN

inverno   *eenvernoh*

WINTER

Monday	lunedì	*loonaydee*
Tuesday	martedì	*martaydee*
Wednesday	mercoledì	*merkolaydee*
Thursday	giovedì	*jovaydee*
Friday	venerdì	*vaynayrdee*
Saturday	sabato	*sabatoh*
Sunday	domenica	*domayneekah*

By the way, school starts at around 8.30 a.m. for most children in Italy and ends around 1.00 p.m., but they also have to go to school on Saturday morning.

Good times

It's ...

Sono ...

💋 sonoh

(five) o'clock

le (cinque)

💋 lay (cheenkway)

quarter after (two)

le (due) e un quarto

💋 lay (dooay) ay oon kwartoh

quarter to (four)

le (quattro) meno un quarto

💋 lay (kwat-troh) maynoh

oon kwartoh

half past (three)

le (tre) e mezzo

💋 lay (tray) ay medzoh

five after (ten)

le (dieci) e cinque

🗣 lay (deeaychee) ay cheenkway

twenty after (eleven)

le (undici) e venti

🗣 lay (oondeechee) ay vayntee

ten to (four)

le (quattro) meno dieci

🗣 lay (kwat-troh) maynoh deeaychee

twenty to (six)

le (sei) meno venti

🗣 lay (say) maynoh vayntee

Watch out for "one o'clock." It's a bit different from the other times. If you want to say "It's one o'clock" you have to say **È l'una** (*ay loonah*). "It's half past one" is **È l'una e mezza** (*ay loonah ay medzah*), and so on.

121

morning
la mattina
👄 lah mat-teenah

midday
mezzogiorno
👄 medzojorrnoh

afternoon
il pomeriggio
👄 eel pomayreedjoh

evening la sera
👄 lah sayrah

midnight
mezzanotte
👄 medzanot-tay

122

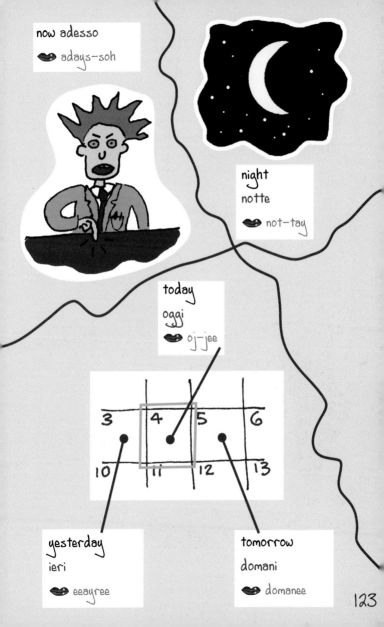

123

Weather wise

Can we go out?
Possiamo uscire?

 pos-seeamoh oosheeray

It's hot
Fa caldo

 fah kaldoh

It's cold
Fa freddo

 fah frayd-doh

It's a horrible day
Fa cattivo tempo

 fa kat-teevoh taympoh

It's raining basins!

When it rains heavily in Italy, people say it's "raining basins": **Piove a catinelle** (*peeovay ah kateenayl-lay*). A well-known saying is **Cielo a pecorelle acqua a catinelle**, or "Small sheep in the sky means basins of water." "Small sheep" are fluffy clouds!

Signs of life

altezza minima
minimum height

Vietato l'uso dei telefonini

Cell phones not allowed

Vietato l'ingresso
No Entry

Vietato ai minori di 18 anni

Under 18s not allowed